STUDY GUIDE

ONE BILLION STARTS WITH ONE

HOW TO SHARE JESUS WITHOUT BEING RELIGIOUS

TIM DILENA

Carpenter's Son Publishing

One Billion Starts with One Study Guide: How to Share Jesus without Being Religious

Published by Carpenter's Son Publishing
Carpentersonpublishing.com

Cover and Interior Design by HybridStudios.com

Printed in the United States of America

ISBN: 978-1-968127-25-1 (print)

STUDY GUIDE

ONE BILLION STARTS WITH ONE

HOW TO SHARE JESUS WITHOUT BEING RELIGIOUS

TIM DILENA

CONTENTS

01 BE SURE YOUR SIN WILL FIND YOU OUT 7

02 I'M NOT ASHAMED, I'M JUST SCARED 13

03 TALKING TO MEN IN DRESSES 19

04 STUCK UPSTAIRS WHEN I SHOULD BE DOWNSTAIRS 25

05 THE FISH ARE FOUND IN THE DEEP 31

06 313 CONVERSATIONS AND CONVERSIONS 37

07 GOING 100 MILES OUT OF THE WAY TO CHANGE THE WORLD 43

08 CAN MY PRAYER LIFE OPEN UP PRISON DOORS? 49

09 A CLEAR VOICE NEEDS A CLEAN HEART 55

10 FIGHT, FIGHT, MIRACLE 61

11 FIRE SNATCHERS 67

12 GO, STAND, SPEAK 73

13 JUST TELL YOUR STORY—THE POWER OF A TESTIMONY 79

14 SPEAKING TO ETERNITY 85

15 LIGHT VERSUS LIGHTING 91

16 REDEFINING VERY GOOD 97

01

BE SURE YOUR SIN WILL FIND YOU OUT

But if you will not do so, behold, you have sinned against the Lord, and be sure your sin will find you out. (Numbers 32:23, ESV)

Sin affects our calling, not our salvation. The "sin that finds you out" is becoming comfortable in your own victory while forgetting others still in need.

In Numbers 32, as Israel prepared to enter Canaan, the tribes of Reuben and Gad wanted to settle east of the Jordan River in Gilead. Moses challenged them:

Shall your brothers go to war while you sit here? (Numbers 32:6).

They promised to help the other tribes secure their inheritance before settling down. Moses agreed but warned that if they abandoned the fight prematurely, their sin would find them out.

QUESTION

Have you ever considered that keeping your spiritual victory to yourself could be a sin? Why might this be true?

____

____

____

POINT 1

WILL YOU FIGHT FOR OTHERS
AFTER WINNING YOUR FIGHT?

> *The greatest single cause of atheism in the world today is Christians: who acknowledge Jesus with their lips, walk out the door, and deny Him by their lifestyle. That is what an unbelieving world simply finds unbelievable.*[1]
> —Brennan Manning

CONCEPT

The sin that will find you out is saying, "I got what I wanted, so I'm done fighting."

INSIGHTS

+ When God blesses us with "houses full of good things" we didn't build, we must not forget He led us out of slavery.
+ God's blessings aren't just for us—they equip us to fight for others still needing freedom.
+ "One of the greatest diseases is to be nobody to anybody." —Attributed to Mother Teresa

DISCUSSION QUESTIONS

Have you ever reached a place where you feel comfortable and just want to settle? What tempts you to stay there?

How can we avoid forgetting where we came from when God blesses us?

What motivates you to step beyond your comfort zone to help others find victory?

POINT 2

WE FIGHT WHEN WE SERVE PEOPLE

> *These people make a big show of saying the right thing, but their heart isn't in it.* (Matthew 15:8, MSG)

CONCEPT

Every act of service creates a place where people can encounter Christ.

INSIGHTS

+ Fighting Through Service: Serving in church creates opportunities for others to encounter Christ.
+ Fighting Through Giving: Our giving supports outreach efforts that spread the gospel.
+ Fighting Through Support: By standing with believers facing persecution around the world, we display our support.

DISCUSSION QUESTION:

How does serving in the church create opportunities for others to encounter Christ and be encouraged in their faith?

____

____

____

____

POINT 3

WE FIGHT WHEN WE SPEAK TO PEOPLE ABOUT ETERNITY

The right words without the right life will send the wrong message.

CONCEPT

Ignoring the spiritual needs of others is a sin of omission.

SCRIPTURE

+ "When you did it to one of the least of these my brothers and sisters, you were doing it to me." (Matthew 25:40)

INSIGHTS

+ The Judgment of the Sheep and Goats: Jesus separates people based on how they treated others.
+ Those who cared for the hungry, naked, sick, and imprisoned were blessed.
+ Serving others is directly serving Christ.

DISCUSSION QUESTIONS

How does the sin of doing nothing affect our ability to share the gospel and care for others in need?

____

____

____

How can we practically live out caring for "the least of these" in our daily lives?

____

____

____

Why is it important to see serving others as a reflection of serving Christ?

____

____

____

____

CONCLUSION

DON'T WADDLE OUT OF HERE TODAY

Let your light shine before others, that they may see your good deeds and glorify your Father in heaven. (Matthew 5:16)

CONCEPT

We are called not just to hear the message but to act on it.

ILLUSTRATION

+ Kierkegaard's Duck Church Ducks gather, hear the message to use their wings, but instead of flying, they simply waddle back to their comfort.[2] Similarly, Christians are called not to just hear the message but to act.

CLOSING

The tribes promised: "We will not return to our homes until every one of the sons of Israel has possessed his inheritance" (Numbers 32:18).

What is your promise to those still waiting for their victory?

02

I'M NOT ASHAMED, I'M JUST SCARED

For I am not ashamed of the gospel of Christ, for it is the power of God to salvation for everyone who believes. (Romans 1:16)

Fear and hesitation often keep us from sharing the gospel. We rely on pastors and churches to do what God has entrusted to every believer. Sharing the good news is not just a leader's responsibility—it's the calling of every Christian.

Paul boldly declared the gospel despite opposition (Romans 1:16). In Acts 17:17, he reasoned with both Jews and Gentiles daily. Proverbs 11:30 reminds us: "He who wins souls is wise."

REFLECTION QUESTION

How has fear or hesitation ever kept you from sharing the gospel?

____

____

____

____

____

POINT 1

DON'T "GO" UNTIL YOU "COME"

> *Come to me, all who labor and are heavy laden, and I will give you rest.* (Matthew 11:28)

CONCEPT

Time with Jesus fuels courage to share the gospel. Lack of prayer often produces hesitancy.

INSIGHTS

+ Prayer strengthens faith and emboldens us to share Christ.
+ Intimacy with Jesus leads naturally to evangelism.
+ A lack of prayer directly weakens our witness.

SCRIPTURES

+ "Go therefore and make disciples of all nations." (Matthew 28:19)
+ "He appointed the twelve that they might be with him and that he might send them out to preach." (Mark 3:14)

DISCUSSION QUESTIONS

What is the power of prayer, and how does it transform the way we approach evangelism?

____

____

____

How can daily prayer prepare you to start and sustain gospel conversations?

____

____

____

POINT 2
STAY ALERT FOR OPEN DOORS

CONCEPT
God provides opportunities to share the gospel—we must stay alert and courageous.

INSIGHTS
+ Open doors are God-appointed opportunities to speak truth.
+ Resistance is normal—fear, doubt, and nervousness will come—but God's strength overcomes them.
+ Boldness creates lasting impact—our courage can change lives.

SCRIPTURES
+ "Devote yourselves to prayer, being watchful and thankful. And pray for us, too, that God may open a door for our message . . ." (Colossians 4:2–5)
+ "Preach the word; be prepared in season and out of season." (2 Timothy 4:2)

DISCUSSION QUESTIONS
How can we recognize and seize God-appointed opportunities to share the gospel?

What are some ways to overcome nervousness and fear when sharing our faith?

How can we be ready to share the gospel, even when it feels inconvenient?

POINT 3

DON'T GO TO BATTLE WITHOUT YOUR SWORD

CONCEPT

The Word of God is our weapon in evangelism—alive, powerful, and transformative.

INSIGHTS

+ God's Word cuts through doubt and defense. (Hebrews 4:12–13)
+ Preaching Scripture in every season carries God's authority.
+ The truth of God's Word breaks lies and transforms lives.
+ "The Word of God is like a lion. You don't have to defend a lion. All you have to do is let the lion loose, and the lion will defend itself."[3]—Charles Spurgeon

DISCUSSION QUESTIONS

How have you experienced the transformative power of God's Word in your life?

What are some ways to prepare yourself to share Scripture with others?

How can we trust God's Word to break through doubts when sharing the gospel?

CONCLUSION

I HAVE NOT HIDDEN THIS GOOD NEWS IN MY HEART!

TAKEAWAY

Evangelism requires prayer, alertness, and reliance on God's Word.

ILLUSTRATION

+ The hymn "I Have Decided to Follow Jesus" was born from the martyrdom of a family in India. Their bold confession—"The cross before me, the world behind me"—inspired an entire village to faith.[4] Their courage stands in contrast to our hesitation.

CLOSING

Who is one person you will commit to pray for and share the gospel with this year?

03

TALKING TO MEN IN DRESSES

I am the Lord your God, who brought you out of the land of Egypt, out of the house of slavery. (Exodus 20:2)

When evangelizing, we must prioritize introducing people to who God is—a loving Father—before discussing His commands. His love transforms His commands from burdens into blessings.

Before giving the Ten Commandments, God reminded Israel of His loving act of deliverance from slavery in Egypt. This context reframes His laws as acts of care, not control.

> *You have only one business and that is the salvation of souls.*[5] —John Wesley

REFLECTION QUESTION

How does understanding God's love change the way we respond to His commands?

____

____

____

POINT 1

THE FOUNDATION OF EVANGELISM: KNOWING THE FATHER

CONCEPT

The foundation of evangelism is introducing people to the heart of the Father.

> *I am the LORD your God, who brought you out of the land of Egypt, out of the house of slavery.* (Exodus 20:2)

INSIGHTS

+ God's commands are rooted in relationship, not control.
+ People reject God's laws because they don't know His love.
+ Evangelism begins with who God is, not what He requires.

DISCUSSION QUESTIONS

How does understanding God's love and deliverance change the way we share the gospel?

____

____

____

How can we introduce people to the heart of God before talking about His commands?

____

____

____

Have you ever had a conversation where someone rejected a biblical principle? How might this approach have changed that?

____

____

____

____

POINT 2

THE POWER OF THE GOSPEL: THE DEATH AND LIFE OF JESUS

CONCEPT

The power of the gospel is revealed in the death and life of Jesus.

SCRIPTURES

+ "For if while we were enemies we were reconciled to God through the death of His Son . . ." (Romans 5:10)
+ "God demonstrates His own love toward us, in that while we were yet sinners, Christ died for us." (Romans 5:6–8)

INSIGHTS

+ God loved us at our worst—before we changed.
+ The cross proves the extent of God's love.
+ Our reconciliation makes us children, not just converts.

DISCUSSION QUESTIONS

How does knowing that God loved you at your worst change the way you see others?

What's the difference between believing Jesus died and believing He died for you personally?

How can we practically share this message with those who feel unworthy of His grace?

POINT 3

FREEDOM LEADS TO FOLLOWING—
OBEDIENCE FLOWS FROM LOVE

ILLUSTRATION

+ The parable of Abraham Lincoln and the freed slave girl: "Then I shall go with you."[6]

INSIGHTS

+ True freedom inspires devotion.
+ We don't follow Jesus because of rules but because of His goodness.
+ Our response to grace is love-driven obedience.

DISCUSSION QUESTIONS

What does the story of the freed slave girl teach us about our response to Christ's sacrifice?

How does understanding our freedom in Christ shape our obedience to Him?

How can you live in a way that reflects love-based obedience this week?

CONCLUSION

BEFORE YOU SHARE WHAT GOD EXPECTS, SHARE WHO HE IS

ILLUSTRATION

+ Tracy and Toya at the soup kitchen asked, "Will we go to heaven like this?" The answer wasn't about rules—it was about knowing God.

SCRIPTURE CONNECTION

Exodus 20:2 reminds us that God's love came before His law.

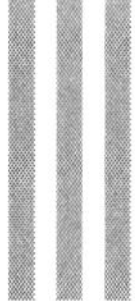

CLOSING

What is your promise to others still waiting for victory—will you lead with God's heart before His commands?

04

STUCK UPSTAIRS WHEN I SHOULD BE DOWNSTAIRS

The Holy Spirit was given to you to walk down the stairs. —Tim Dilena

The Great Commission isn't just for pastors—it's for every believer. We must leave the safety of our "upper room" experiences and step into the real world to bring the gospel to those who may never walk into a church.

After the outpouring of the Holy Spirit in Acts 2, the disciples didn't stay secluded. They stepped into the streets (see Acts 3), where miracles and multiplication happened, fulfilling Jesus' command in Matthew 28.

REFLECTION QUESTION

Where is God asking you to "come downstairs" and bring His presence into the world?

____

____

____

POINT 1

GOD USES 3 P.M. CHRISTIANS

> *Peter and John were going up to the temple at the ninth hour, the hour of prayer.* (Acts 3:1)

CONCEPT

Ordinary people with daily routines can experience extraordinary moments when they walk in the Spirit.

QUOTES

+ Tim Dilena: "The church is living, and living things move."

+ "Acts 3 determines if Acts 2 was real."[7]

INSIGHTS

+ Spiritual power must move from the upper room to the street.

+ God often moves through our regular routines.

+ The miracle happened on the street, not in the sanctuary.

DISCUSSION QUESTIONS

What does being a "3 P.M. Christian" mean to you?

____

____

Who in your life is waiting for the church to "come downstairs"?

____

____

____

How can your daily schedule become a mission field?

____

____

____

POINT 2

GOD WILL GIVE YOU NEW EYES WHEN YOU COME DOWNSTAIRS

CONCEPT

Spiritual revival changes how we see people and opportunities.

SCRIPTURES

+ "Peter . . . fixed his gaze on him and said, 'Look at us!'" (Acts 3:2–4)

+ Acts 4:4—The miracle became the platform for multiplication.

QUOTES

+ "It's not a true work of God if you don't treat people better afterward."

+ D. L. Moody: "I like my way of doing it better than your way of not doing it."[8]

INSIGHTS

+ Revival leads to compassion and boldness.

+ We often overlook what God is asking us to see.

+ Spiritual sight allows us to see potential where others see problems.

DISCUSSION QUESTIONS

Who have you passed by that God wants you to "see"?

How can asking "Can I pray with you?" open doors this week?

What does it mean to have "new eyes" in your spiritual life?

POINT 3

THE BAPTISM OF THE HOLY SPIRIT CHANGES EVERYTHING

CONCEPT

The Holy Spirit empowers us for action, not just personal experiences.

SCRIPTURES

+ "You will receive power . . ." (Acts 1:8)
+ " . . . they were filled with the Holy Spirit and spoke the word

of God with boldness." (Acts 4:31)

QUOTES

+ "The Holy Spirit was given to you to walk down the stairs." —Tim Dilena
+ "I really felt I did not want to live if I could not have this power for service." —D. L. Moody[9]

INSIGHTS

+ The Holy Spirit empowers you to witness boldly.
+ The goal of baptism in the Spirit is obedience and outreach.
+ Small acts of obedience create space for great moves of God.

DISCUSSION QUESTIONS

How has the Holy Spirit changed your ministry or daily life?

____

____

____

What is one comfort-zone habit you can replace with prayer this week?

____

____

Where do you need the Spirit's boldness most right now?

____

____

CONCLUSION

TAKEAWAY

The power of the upper room is meant for the streets below.

ILLUSTRATION

+ David Wilkerson's small act of obedience (selling his TV) led to a global ministry.[10]
+ A post on the Church Gist Facebook page in December 201 included the statement, "Grenada prison ministry—bringing the church to those who couldn't come upstairs."

SCRIPTURE CONNECTION

"The Word became flesh and dwelt among us." (John 1:14)

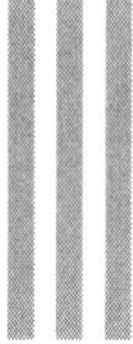

CLOSING

Where is God asking you to go that your comfort zone has kept you from?

THE FISH ARE FOUND IN THE DEEP

They signaled to their partners in the other boat . . . and they came and helped them. (Luke 5:7)

God is calling us out of comfort and into deep waters. Like Peter, we must say yes to Jesus even when it doesn't make sense. The deep is risky, but it's where lives are changed, souls are saved, and stories are rewritten. The miracle isn't at the shore—it's in the deep.

In Luke 5, Jesus calls Peter to fish again—after a night of failure. Obedience despite confusion opens the door to a new purpose: "From now on, you will be catching men" (v.10). Jeremiah 16 adds that God is always writing new stories—and He wants to do that through us.

REFLECTION QUESTION

Where is God calling you to go deeper with Him, even if it feels uncomfortable or uncertain?

POINT 1
YOU NEED OBEDIENCE

At Your bidding, I will let down the nets. (Luke 5:4–5)

CONCEPT
God's commands often defy logic—but miracles follow obedience.

QUOTES
+ "The catcher of fish is not smarter than the Creator of fish."
+ "We dangerously rely on our experience instead of His omniscience."

INSIGHTS
+ Obedience is the first step toward the miraculous.
+ Jesus often calls us to act when it feels least logical.
+ One step of obedience can launch a legacy.

ILLUSTRATIONS
+ David Wilkerson obeyed God's call to reach gang members, eventually leading to Sonny Arguinzoni's transformation and global ministry.[11]
+ *We Bought a Zoo* quote: "Sometimes all you need is 20 seconds of insane courage."[12]
+ Steve Jobs to John Sculley: "Do you want to sell sugared water . . . or change the world?"[13]

DISCUSSION QUESTIONS
Where is God calling you to obey despite logic or past failure?

What small step of obedience have you taken that led to a big impact?

What internal resistance do you face when struggling to obey God?

POINT 2
YOU NEED NETS

> *If you don't open your mouth in church, you won't open it in the world.*

CONCEPT
Your "net" is your voice—you must speak to share Jesus.

SCRIPTURES
+ "How will they hear without a preacher?" (Romans 10:14, 17)
+ "Let the redeemed of the Lord say so." (Psalm 107:2)

INSIGHTS
+ The gospel spreads through speaking, not silence.

+ We must move beyond good intentions into bold proclamation.

+ Everyone has a "net"—testimony, influence, creativity—so use it.

ILLUSTRATIONS

+ Ezra reading Scripture stirred hearts as people responded aloud. (Nehemiah 8)

+ Maria, once homeless, became a pastor—because someone brought sandwiches, rubbing alcohol, and the gospel.

+ According to many prominent members of the Christian community, "The Church has lost its voice"—but revival begins when we speak up.

DISCUSSION QUESTIONS

In what ways is God calling you to be more vocal about your faith?

____

____

What unique "net" has God placed in your hands, and are you using it?

____

____

____

What fears or doubts stop you from opening your mouth?

____

____

POINT 3

YOU NEED HELP

One boat got the call, the other got the catch. Both were needed.

CONCEPT

You can't go deep alone—the harvest requires community.

SCRIPTURES

+ "They signaled their partners . . ." (Luke 5:7)
+ "We are God's fellow workers." (1 Corinthians 3:9)

INSIGHTS

+ Deep-water fishing leads to overflow—you need others to help gather.
+ Evangelism isn't solo—it's teamwork.
+ You may support the miracle, even if you're not the one who receives it.

ILLUSTRATIONS

+ "It takes ten people to lead one person to Christ." —Attributed to Billy Graham
+ *Karate Kid* metaphor: God's prep often feels mundane, but it's strategic.
+ Maria's transformation required years of love from many people.

DISCUSSION QUESTIONS

Who encourages your faith, and who might God be asking you

to encourage?

Are you willing to be a "supporting boat," even without recognition?

CONCLUSION

TAKEAWAY

The miracle of the deep requires obedience, your voice, and partnership. Jesus doesn't just step into any boat—He chooses the one that's available.

SCRIPTURE CONNECTION

"He saw two boats . . . and got into one." (Luke 5:2–3)

Jeremiah 16:14–15: God is still writing new stories—will you be part of one?

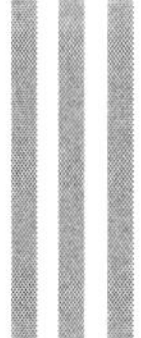

CLOSING

Would He choose your boat? Are you positioned, surrendered, and ready?

06

313 CONVERSATIONS AND CONVERSIONS

This is a day of good news and we aren't sharing it with anyone . . . (2 Kings 7:9)

Evangelism isn't just for Sundays—it's for the 313 other days we live in neighborhoods, offices, and ordinary spaces. Joseph's story in Genesis 40 shows us that God uses everyday conversations to open doors for salvation. Evangelism begins with observing others, asking questions, and letting God guide the conversation.

Joseph, imprisoned in Egypt, noticed the sadness of two men and engaged them in conversation, pointing them toward God. In the same way, we are called to notice the people around us and let holy conversations lead to conversions.

REFLECTION QUESTION

Where is your "elevator"—the everyday space where God may be calling you to share the gospel outside of church?

____

____

____

POINT 1
OBSERVE

CONCEPT
Evangelism often begins not with speaking, but with seeing. Awareness opens the door for holy conversations.

INSIGHTS
+ Joseph noticed the sadness of the cupbearer and baker. (Genesis 40:6)
+ Observation helps us discern people's emotional and spiritual needs.
+ Being attentive positions us to respond with compassion.

ILLUSTRATION
+ According to legend, a Salvation Army worker recognized an older, disfigured woman as someone once sculpted as "Diana" for Madison Square Garden. Observation revealed her story and worth.

DISCUSSION QUESTIONS
How might God be prompting you to notice the needs of people around you?

____

____

____

____

____

____

Who is someone in your daily life you need to pay closer attention to this week?

____

____

____

____

POINT 2
ASK QUESTIONS

> *Let the mouth speak, and the heart will eventually be revealed.* —Tim Dilena

CONCEPT
Questions create space for people to open their hearts. They show care and invite God's work in the conversation.

INSIGHTS
+ Joseph asked, "Why are your faces so sad today?" (Genesis 40:7)
+ Genuine questions invite vulnerability and reveal deeper needs.
+ Jesus often used questions to engage and lead people.

ILLUSTRATION
+ Dr. Francis Collins, head of the Human Genome Project, came to faith after a dying Christian woman asked him one question: "What do you believe?"[14]

QUOTE

"He who asks the questions controls the conversation."

DISCUSSION QUESTIONS

Why do you think Jesus used questions so often?

Has a sincere question ever opened the door for you—or someone else—to faith?

POINT 3

BRING IN THE GOD PART

CONCEPT

After trust is built, we must point people to God. We are not the answer—we carry the answer.

INSIGHTS

+ Joseph said, "Do not interpretations belong to God? Tell it to me, please." (Genesis 40:8)

+ The "God part" may take time, but persistence pays off.
+ Faith conversations flow naturally when we've observed and listened well.

ILLUSTRATION

+ Tim Dilena shared the story of Hung, a dry cleaner in Detroit. After ten years of kind conversations, Hung eventually came to Christ.

DISCUSSION QUESTIONS

How can you recognize the right moment to bring God into a conversation?

____

____

____

What are simple, natural ways to introduce faith without being forced?

____

____

____

____

CONCLUSION

TAKEAWAY

Evangelism is not about sermons but about holy conversations. Observe, ask, and bring in the God part.

ILLUSTRATION

+ John Harper on the *Titanic* handed out life jackets and shouted the gospel until his dying breath.[15] Evangelism is about making every moment count for eternity.

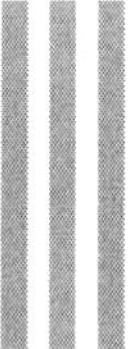

CLOSING

What is one conversation you can have this week that could point someone toward Christ?

07

CAN MY PRAYER LIFE OPEN UP PRISON DOORS?

But prayer for him was being made fervently by the church to God. (Acts 12:5)

Prayer is not just a discipline—it is a weapon of spiritual warfare. In Acts 12, Peter's release from prison came through fervent prayer. The destiny of people and the advance of God's kingdom are tied to the prayers of the church. Someone's freedom might depend on your prayer life.

James was executed, but Peter was spared. The difference was the church's fervent intercession. Prayer shifted the outcome, proving that when God's people pray, prison doors open.

REFLECTION QUESTION

Do you see prayer as optional or essential? How might your prayers be the key to someone else's breakthrough?

POINT 1

FERVENT PRAYER CHANGES THE OUTCOME

CONCEPT

Prayer isn't polite—it's fervent. Four words, "But prayer for him . . . ," changed Peter's story.

INSIGHTS

+ God responds to faith-filled, stretched-out prayer.
+ The church's desperation led to divine intervention.
+ Prayer can shift the trajectory of lives, families, and communities.

SCRIPTURE

+ "So Peter was kept in the prison, but prayer for him was being made fervently by the church to God." (Acts 12:5)

ILLUSTRATION

+ Tim Dilena recounted a debate with a professor who denied that prayer changes outcomes. Scripture proves otherwise: Peter lived because the church prayed.

DISCUSSION QUESTIONS

Have you ever seen prayer shift defeat into breakthrough?

___

___

___

___

Where is God calling you to "stretch out" in prayer this week?

____

____

____

POINT 2

CHAINS FALL AND PRISON DOORS OPEN WHEN WE PRAY

> *The effectual fervent prayer of a righteous man avails much.* (James 5:16)

CONCEPT

Prayer is a weapon that breaks chains, opens doors, and sets captives free.

INSIGHTS

+ Political power and human effort couldn't stop God's intervention.
+ Fervent prayer unleashes angelic activity and divine deliverance.
+ Specific, faith-filled prayer changes stories.

SCRIPTURE

Acts 12:6–11: The angel appears, chains fall, and Peter walks free.

ILLUSTRATION

+ Michele was healed from stage 4 liver disease after a prayer during an online service. Prayer still opens prison doors today.

DISCUSSION QUESTIONS

Where do you see "prison doors" that need to be opened in your life or family?

____

____

____

____

How does Peter's deliverance encourage you to pray boldly this week?

____

____

____

POINT 3

THE HARVEST AND THE BATTLE BELONG TO THOSE WHO PRAY

> *To get nations back on their feet, we must first get the church down on its knees.*—Attributed to Billy Graham

CONCEPT

Prayer fuels revival and the harvest of souls. Without prayer, the mission stalls.

INSIGHTS

+ Jesus connected the harvest to intercessors. (Matthew 9:36–38)
+ Revivals begin with prayer, not programs.

+ Tools without prayer are powerless—prayer is the bow that launches the battle.

ILLUSTRATIONS

+ The Hebrides Revival began with two elderly women who refused to stop praying.[16]

+ Ephraim had weapons but failed to fight—reminding us that unused prayer is wasted power.

QUOTE

+ “History is silent about revivals that did not begin with prayer.” —Attributed to revival historian J. Edwin Orr.

DISCUSSION QUESTIONS

Who are you praying for that needs salvation?

____

____

____

____

____

____

What area of your life requires you to persist in prayer for souls?

____

____

____

____

____

CONCLUSION

TAKEAWAY

Your prayers matter—prison doors open, chains fall, and revival begins when God's people pray.

ILLUSTRATION

+ The Hebrides Revival shows that even hidden prayers can shake nations. The church in Acts proves prayer shifts destinies.

CLOSING

Are you willing to fight your battles on your knees so that others can walk free?

08

A CLEAR VOICE NEEDS A CLEAN HEART

Let the words of my mouth and the meditation of my heart be acceptable in Your sight, O Lord. (Psalm 19:14)

Our mission to reach the lost begins with our own hearts. Psalm 51 reminds us that a clean heart is the key to a clear voice—a voice that can pray, worship, and witness with power. Hidden sin, even when small, silences us. God's conviction is not punishment, but preparation for what He wants to do through us.

David's sin cost him his voice in three areas: intercession, praise, and testimony. Only after repentance was he restored to pray for others, worship authentically, and witness boldly.

REFLECTION QUESTION

Is there any hidden sin in your life that is silencing your voice for God?

____

____

____

POINT 1

SIN SILENCES OUR INTERCESSION

> *Create in me a clean heart . . . restore* to me . . .
> (Psalm 51:10–12)

CONCEPT

Sin pulls our prayers inward, making them self-focused. Instead of interceding for others, we get trapped in praying only for ourselves.

INSIGHTS

+ David's prayer in Psalm 51 was consumed with "me" and "my."

+ Sin shifts our focus away from others' needs.

+ Intercession regains power when the heart is cleansed.

SCRIPTURE

"Be gracious to me . . . wash me . . . cleanse me." (Psalm 51:1–3)

ILLUSTRATION

+ David, a king and shepherd of Israel, could no longer intercede for his people while trapped in hidden sin.

DISCUSSION QUESTIONS

Why do you think sin makes our prayers self-focused?

Who in your life needs your intercession this week?

____

____

____

____

____

POINT 2
SIN SILENCES OUR PRAISE

CONCEPT
Sin drains the fire from our worship, leaving only empty songs. True praise flows from a clean heart.

INSIGHTS
+ David, known for his worship, lost his voice of praise until he repented.

+ Worship without purity is noise; worship with repentance is joy.

+ A clean heart revives authentic adoration.

SCRIPTURE
+ "Deliver me . . . then my tongue will joyfully sing of Your righteousness." (Psalm 51:14)

ILLUSTRATION
+ David, the psalmist-king, was silent before God until he confessed and was cleansed.

DISCUSSION QUESTIONS

Have you experienced worship that felt empty because of unconfessed sin?

____

____

____

____

What area of your life might God want to cleanse so your praise can be genuine?

____

____

____

____

POINT 3

SIN SILENCES OUR TESTIMONY

> *Then I will teach transgressors Your ways, and sinners shall be converted to You.* (Psalm 51:13)

CONCEPT

Sin robs us of the power to share the gospel. A guilty heart cannot speak boldly.

INSIGHTS

+ David prayed in Psalm 51:13 that after restoration he could teach sinners again.

+ Sin steals confidence and credibility.
+ God restores our testimony so we can point others to Him.

ILLUSTRATION

+ Even those who know much Scripture can remain silent if sin is left unchecked. A clean heart restores a bold voice.

DISCUSSION QUESTIONS

Have you ever felt disqualified from sharing your faith because of sin?

____

____

____

____

____

How does God's compassion in Nehemiah 9 encourage you to share your testimony again?

____

____

____

____

CONCLUSION

TAKEAWAY

A clean heart leads to a clear voice—for intercession, praise, and testimony. Sin silences us, but repentance restores us.

ILLUSTRATIONS

- The Garbage Barge:[17] Sin weighs us down until we dump it at Jesus' feet.
- The Dentist's Chair: God doesn't just relieve symptoms; He restores us completely.

CLOSING

Is your heart clean so your voice can be clear?

09

FIGHT, FIGHT, MIRACLE

A rich man's wealth is his strong city,
And like a high wall in his own imagination.
(Proverbs 18:11, NASB)

The work of winning souls isn't always quick or clean. It can feel like loss after loss, resistance, or discouraging conversations. Yet, these are not defeats—they are part of God's divine strategy. In Judges 20, Israel lost twice despite following God's direction, but each fight was positioning them for a miracle. Likewise, every failed attempt at reaching someone for Christ may be God luring them out from behind their walls. Our call is simple: fight, fight, miracle.

> *And if I may put it this way . . . I miss Him.*[18]
> —Charles Templeton in interview with Lee Strobel

ILLUSTRATION

+ David Wilkerson faced rejection after rejection from Nicky Cruz before his conversion. What looked like failure was actually God's setup. Fight, fight, miracle.

REFLECTION QUESTION

How do you typically interpret resistance when you share your faith—with discouragement, or with expectation of what God may be setting up?

POINT 1

FAILED BATTLES ARE PART OF THE STRATEGY

> *Sometimes the green light leads to a fight, not a finish line.*—Tim Dilena

CONCEPT

Obedience doesn't guarantee immediate success. Israel obeyed God and still lost twice. But God was not absent—He was preparing them for a miracle. Setbacks are often setups in God's plan.

SCRIPTURE

+ Judges 20:18–21: God told Judah to go first, but Israel lost 22,000 men.

ILLUSTRATION

+ Israel's early defeats exposed the enemy's position and set the stage for victory.

DISCUSSION QUESTIONS

Have you ever obeyed God and still felt defeated? How did that affect your faith?

Why might God allow us to lose battles on the way to winning the war?

POINT 2

WORLDVIEWS ARE WALLS

> *A rich man's wealth is his strong city, And like a high wall in his own imagination.* (Proverbs 18:11)

CONCEPT

People rarely reject the gospel because of logic—it's often because of deep-rooted worldviews that act like fortresses. These walls, built from pain, pride, or disappointment, keep God at a distance. But truth, spoken consistently and compassionately, creates cracks in the wall.

ILLUSTRATION

+ Charles Templeton, after decades of resistance, admitted in tears, "I miss Him."[19] Behind walls of doubt, his heart still longed for Christ.

QUOTE

+ "Truth creates cracks in the walls people hide behind."—Tim Dilena

DISCUSSION QUESTIONS

What kinds of "walls" do you see people build against God—intellectual, emotional, or cultural?

How can we gently dismantle strongholds without turning evangelism into an argument?

When have you seen persistence in love start to break down someone's defenses?

POINT 3

MIRACLES FOLLOW THE FIGHT

> *Go up, for tomorrow I will deliver them into your hand.* (Judges 20:28)

CONCEPT

Victory came for Israel not after the first or second battle, but after prayer, fasting, and perseverance. Miracles often follow testing and endurance. Fight, fight, miracle is not failure—it's divine strategy.

CHAPTER 09

SCRIPTURE

"And the LORD struck Benjamin before Israel . . . " (Judges 20:35)

QUOTE

+ "Fight, fight, miracle isn't failure, it's divine strategy." —Tim Dilena

ILLUSTRATION

+ David Wilkerson's persistence with Nicky Cruz and Amy's 23 years of prayer for her mother both remind us that miracles are often delayed but never denied.

DISCUSSION QUESTIONS

How do you tell the difference between a delayed miracle and a closed door?

____

____

____

What keeps you pressing on when it feels like nothing is changing?

____

____

____

Who are you fighting for right now that requires "fight, fight, miracle" faith?

____

____

____

CONCLUSION

TAKEAWAY

Pray daily for someone you're believing for. Ask God to show you their walls and reveal cracks where truth can enter.

Don't quit. Every loss may be part of God's larger plan. Keep fighting, because the miracle is coming.

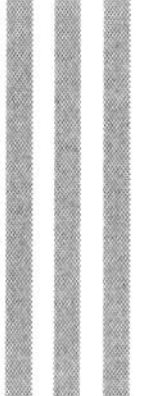

CLOSING

Revisit Judges 20 and reflect: Am I in the "fight" phase right now, waiting for God's miracle?

GOING 100 MILES OUT OF THE WAY TO CHANGE THE WORLD

Those who had been scattered went about preaching the word. Philip went down to Samaria and proclaimed Christ. (Acts 8:4–5)

This message invites us to embrace divine interruptions—those inconvenient nudges from the Holy Spirit that lead to life-changing conversations. From Acts 8, Philip left a revival in Samaria to travel one hundred miles on a desert road for one man: an Ethiopian eunuch. That encounter launched the gospel into Africa.

We often don't see the full picture when God nudges us. Obedience in small, inconvenient moments is what opens the door to miracles and eternal impact. Interruptions are not accidents; they are sacred opportunities.

> *Proclaim the Word . . . when it is convenient and when it is not.* (2 Timothy 4:2, TPT)

QUOTES

+ "We believe up to the point of inconvenience."
  —Attributed to Leonard Ravenhill
+ "These elevator conversations are what Paul called 'Being

instant in season and out of season.'" —Tim Dilena

+ "God uses a persecution, a waiter, and an outcast people to bring the first revival outside of Jerusalem." —Tim Dilena
+ "You don't get Africa if you don't go to the desert road." —Tim Dilena

ILLUSTRATIONS

+ Tim Dilena's "elevator apology" story with Jason
+ Edward Kimball's witness to D. L. Moody[20]
+ O. S. Hawkins sharing the gospel with a waiter[21]

DISCUSSION QUESTION

How do you usually respond when the Holy Spirit nudges you at inconvenient times? What holds you back?

____

____

POINT 1

THE NUDGE (OBEDIENCE)

> *The Spirit said to Philip, "Go up and join this chariot."* (Acts 8:29)

CONCEPT

Obedience begins by saying "yes" to divine interruptions. Philip left revival on just a nudge from God. Many divine moments are missed because they don't fit our schedule or comfort zone.

SCRIPTURE

"An angel of the Lord said . . . 'Go to the desert road.' So he went." (Acts 8:26–27)

QUOTES

+ "The nudge of the Holy Spirit happens out of season." —Tim Dilena
+ "You can't behold the potential miracle without a desert road of obedience."

ILLUSTRATIONS

+ Healing of an elder's shoulder during worship
+ Nudge to pray for a Muslim woman at Liberty University

DISCUSSION QUESTIONS

What fears or distractions cause you to hesitate when God nudges you?

____

____

____

____

Can you recall a time when obedience to a nudge led to an unexpected impact?

____

____

____

____

POINT 2

THE TALK (FAITH)

CONCEPT

Faith takes the nudge and turns it into a conversation. Philip risked awkwardness and simply asked, "Do you understand what you're reading?" Gospel conversations often begin with a question, not a sermon.

> *When you do what God wants you to do, there will always be a "behold."* —Tim Dilena

SCRIPTURES

+ "Do you understand what you are reading? . . . 'How could I, unless someone guides me?'" (Acts 8:30–31)
+ Acts 8:32–33: Isaiah's prophecy of Jesus' suffering

SAMPLE QUESTIONS TO START CONVERSATIONS

+ "Do you know God loves you?"
+ "Can I pray for you?"
+ "What do you think happens after we die?"

DISCUSSION QUESTIONS

How can thoughtful, Spirit-led questions become powerful tools for evangelism?

Which question feels most natural for you to ask, and in what setting?

POINT 3

THE POSSIBILITY (THE MIRACLE)

CONCEPT

+ When obedience and faith meet, God works miracles. Philip baptized the eunuch, who carried the gospel to Africa. One conversation on a desert road multiplied into a continent-shaking revival.

> *Then Philip opened his mouth, and beginning with this Scripture he told him the good news about Jesus. And as they were going along the road they came to some water, and the eunuch said, "See, here is water! What prevents me from being baptized?" And he commanded the chariot to stop, and they both went down into the water, Philip and the eunuch, and he baptized him.* (Acts 8:35–38)

HISTORICAL IMPACT

1900—10 million Christians in Africa

1950—50 million

2000—400 million

Today—730+ million across 54 nations[22]

ILLUSTRATIONS

+ The Ethiopian eunuch's conversion and baptism

DISCUSSION QUESTIONS

What does this story teach us about the hidden potential in the people around us?

How can we better recognize and respond when someone is ready to take a spiritual step?

CONCLUSION

CONCEPT

Philip's message to the eunuch was simple: "Jesus." Through Isaiah 53, we are reminded that Jesus—like a lamb led to slaughter—took our place. The gospel isn't just a sermon; it's a mission we live out. The Holy Spirit still nudges. Interruptions are still divine opportunities.

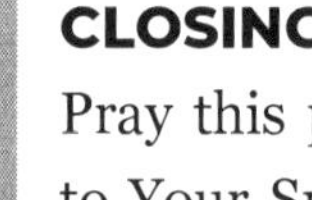

CLOSING

Pray this prayer: "Speak to me, Lord. I want to be sensitive to Your Spirit. Interrupt my plans. I want to follow You, no matter the cost."

This week, ask God for one "chariot moment" where you can step out in faith.

FIRE SNATCHERS

The effective prayer of a righteous man can accomplish much. (James 5:16)

The Bible speaks of a fire beyond natural flames—the fire of sin's destruction. As believers, we are called to be "fire snatchers," spiritual hotshots trained to run into danger to pull people from sin's grip. Jude urges us: "save others, snatching them out of the fire." Fire snatching means urgency, courage, and love that refuses to leave anyone behind.

> *Put your ear down to the Bible, and hear Him bid you go and pull sinners out of the fire of sin.*[23] —William Booth

ILLUSTRATIONS

+ Hotshot firefighters risking their lives in real flames
+ John Wesley: called himself "a brand plucked from the fire" after being rescued as a child[24]
+ Vincent Anderson: healed in faith during a livestream
+ Afghanistan testimony: TSC's Farsi channel as a spiritual lifeline

REFLECTION QUESTION

Who in your life right now is trapped in a fire that God may be calling you to help rescue?

____

____

____

POINT 1

GET ALL THE HELP YOU NEED

CONCEPT

Fire snatching is not a solo mission. Abraham gathered 318 men to rescue Lot. Likewise, we need spiritual reinforcements—intercessors, mentors, and fellow believers—to pull others from the flames.

SCRIPTURE

+ "When Abram heard that his relative had been taken captive, he led out his trained men, born in his house, three hundred and eighteen . . ." (Genesis 14:14)

ILLUSTRATION

+ "Bob" was pulled out of a crack house by Tim Dilena and two brothers in Christ. Rescue required community courage.

DISCUSSION QUESTIONS

Who are the "318" people you can call on to help in spiritual battles?

____

____

____

What holds you back from asking for help in these rescue missions?

____

____

____

POINT 2

DON'T JUST GET ANYONE—GET THE TRAINED

CONCEPT

Some fires require more than good intentions—they demand people trained in prayer, fasting, deliverance, and discernment.

> *He led out his trained men . . .* (Genesis 14:14)

ILLUSTRATION

+ Ministries like Teen Challenge and Victory Outreach equip believers to face fierce fires of addiction and bondage.

QUOTE

+ "Don't use people who know about Freud but not about Lucifer." —Tim Dilena

DISCUSSION QUESTIONS

What does it mean to be spiritually trained for these kinds of battles?

____

____

____

____

Who around you is equipped to help, and how can you learn from them?

POINT 3

GET THE BORN-AGAIN

CONCEPT

To pull someone from fire, you must be alive in Christ. Skill is not enough—you need the Spirit.

SCRIPTURES

+ . . . trained men, born in his house . . . (Genesis 14:14)
+ "The effective prayer of a righteous man can accomplish much." (James 5:16)

ILLUSTRATION

+ Vincent Anderson's healing after raising his hands in faith during livestream prayer—a testimony of Spirit-born authority.

"You need people who carry two birth certificates." —Tim Dilena

DISCUSSION QUESTION

Why is it essential for fire snatchers to be born again, and how can you grow into that kind of spiritual authority?

POINT 4
PURSUE, DON'T WAIT TO BE ASKED

CONCEPT

Lot never called Abraham for help—but Abraham pursued him anyway. True love doesn't wait for an invitation; it moves toward the fire.

> *. . . pulling them out of the fire . . .* (Jude 1:23)

ILLUSTRATION

+ On the 7-train, Tim Dilena stepped into a tense moment to bring peace and witness to Christ.

QUOTE

+ "The longer you wait out the fire, the more it can consume them." —Tim Dilena

DISCUSSION QUESTION

What would it look like to pursue someone in danger before they even ask for help?

____

____

____

POINT 5
EVERY FIGHT IS A NIGHT FIGHT

CONCEPT

Spiritual battles are often waged in darkness. Abraham attacked at night, showing us that prayer is the way to fight when circumstances are unclear.

SCRIPTURES

+ "He divided his forces against them by night . . ." (Genesis 14:15)
+ Genesis 19:29—God remembered Abraham and rescued Lot.

The only way to fight a night fight is with prayer—and sometimes you have to pray them out. —Tim Dilena

DISCUSSION QUESTION

Why is prayer so essential in midnight battles? How have you seen it turn the tide in someone's life?

____

____

CONCLUSION

FIRE SNATCHERS NEEDED

CONCEPT

God is raising up fire snatchers—believers trained, born again, equipped, urgent, and prayer-fueled. Like Abraham, we run into danger for the sake of others, trusting God to rescue through us.

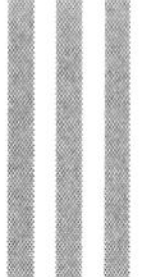

CLOSING

Pray for a burden for those trapped in sin or despair. Ask God to make you a fire snatcher, bold and Spirit-empowered.

12

GO STAND SPEAK (THAT'S WHAT COMES AFTER FREEDOM)

We must obey God rather than men. (Acts 5:29)

After Jesus sets us free, His call is not for passivity or safety—it is to go, stand, and speak. The Christian life is not a merry-go-round but a rollercoaster, with both highs and lows. Through it all, God calls us to obedience, courage, and boldness. Fear is the enemy of our calling, but when we realize God is with us, we find the authority and faith to live boldly. One believer, one step of obedience, can unleash multiplication in families, cities, and even nations.

QUOTES

+ "Go, stand, and speak, that's what comes after freedom." —Tim Dilena
+ "One soul-winner, one conversation, one unsaved person—God can start a multiplication effect." —Tim Dilena
+ "Everything you want and everything you don't have is outside your comfort zone." —Tim Dilena
+ "Fear stops us from going, standing, and speaking." —Tim Dilena

+ “A fanatic is someone who can’t change his mind and won’t change the subject.” —Attributed to Winston Churchill

ILLUSTRATIONS

+ Rollercoaster vs. merry-go-round: faith requires courage to ride with Jesus.

+ Preaching at a firefighter’s funeral after 9/11 opened doors for gospel impact.

+ The apostles’ flogging mirrors modern scrutiny—faith often brings shame in the world’s eyes but honor before God.

REFLECTION QUESTION

Where has fear, comfort, or timidity held you back from going, standing, or speaking for Christ?

____

____

____

____

POINT 1

GO—THAT’S FAITH

CONCEPT

To “go” is to step out in faith, beyond comfort or familiarity. Obedience may feel risky, but every small step can have multiplying impact.

> *Go therefore and make disciples of all nations . . .*
> (Matthew 28:19)

QUOTE

+ "Everything you want and everything you don't have is outside your comfort zone." —Tim Dilena

ILLUSTRATION

+ Tim Dilena's gym encounter: Obedience to go back and check on a friend led to a spiritual conversation.

DISCUSSION QUESTIONS

When have you sensed God prompting you to step out of your comfort zone, and what happened as you obeyed?

____

____

____

Where might God be asking you to "go" this week?

____

____

____

POINT 2

STAND—THAT'S AUTHORITY

CONCEPT

To "stand" is to take your place in God's authority, even when facing opposition. Standing is more than posture—it is a spiritual decision rooted in allegiance to God over people.

SCRIPTURES

+ "We must obey God rather than men." (Acts 5:29)
+ Ezekiel 2:1–2—"Son of man, stand on your feet, and I will speak to you."

You have enemies? Good. That means you've stood up for something. —Victor Hugo

ILLUSTRATION

+ Bringing a physical Bible into pro sports chapels as a bold declaration of allegiance to Christ.

DISCUSSION QUESTIONS

Where is God calling you to take a stand, even if it brings discomfort or misunderstanding?

____

____

____

____

____

How can you surround yourself with people who strengthen your resolve to stand for Christ?

____

____

____

____

____

POINT 3

SPEAK—THAT'S BOLDNESS

CONCEPT

To "speak" is to move from private conviction to public declaration. God fills our mouths when we speak in faith. Speaking up unleashes His power and invites transformation.

SCRIPTURES

+ "Open wide your mouth and I will fill it." (Psalm 81:10)
+ Acts 5:41–42: The apostles rejoiced in suffering and kept preaching daily.

QUOTE

+ "Fear stops us from going, standing, and speaking." —Tim Dilena

ILLUSTRATION

+ Tim Dilena's encounter with a musician: God gave him words in the moment, proving that the Spirit meets us in obedience.

DISCUSSION QUESTIONS

Have you ever shared your faith while feeling nervous or unprepared? How did God meet you?

____

____

____

What fears most often keep you from speaking about Jesus?

CONCLUSION

CONCEPT

The call after freedom is not passivity but obedience: Go. Stand. Speak. Fear is infectious, but so is faith. God is with us in every season—on the rollercoaster ups and downs—and one step of obedience can unleash multiplication for the Kingdom.

CLOSING

Pray for boldness to tell your story with clarity and humility. Ask God to use your testimony to break lies, stir faith, and bring salvation.

Write out your testimony this week with Jesus at the center.

Pray for an opportunity to share it with someone who needs hope.

13

JUST TELL YOUR STORY: THE POWER OF A TESTIMONY

Speak out for Him, to tell others of the night-and-day difference He made for you, from nothing to something . . . (1 Peter 2:9–10, MSG)

God doesn't waste your lowest places. He turns your rock bottom into a pathway of miracles, not only for you but for others. The darkest, most hopeless seasons—the "great deep"—become highways for redemption in His hands. Your testimony is not just your story; it is a road others can travel to find hope, healing, and salvation. The burden for a billion souls begins with one testimony: yours.

The power of a testimony isn't in how dramatic it is, but in how clearly it points to Christ. Whether rescued from deep brokenness or raised in the church, every believer's story is a miracle of grace. When you tell it, you crush lies, break chains, and open doors. Don't hold back. Just tell your story.

SCRIPTURES

- "Was it not You who dried up the sea . . . Who made the depths a pathway for the redeemed?" (Isaiah 51:10)
- "We can't keep quiet about what we've seen and

heard." (Acts 4:20)

+ "Speak out for Him, to tell others of the night-and-day difference He made for you." (1 Peter 2:9–10)

+ "They overcame him by the blood of the Lamb and the word of their testimony." (Revelation 12:11)

+ "One thing I do know. I was blind but now I see!" (John 9:25)

QUOTES

+ "Your testimony has Satan-defeating power. It crushes the enemy's number one weapon, his lies."—Tim Dilena

+ "Don't complicate it, just tell your story. I was blind, but now I see."—Tim Dilena

ILLUSTRATIONS

+ Olympic diver: He was saved physically and spiritually after recalling a friend's simple testimony.

+ Detroit motel: A pimp and a drug dealer were radically saved, proving no one is too far gone.

+ Nicky Cruz: For decades, his testimony has changed millions of lives.

REFLECTION QUESTION

What part of your story is God asking you to share so that others may find freedom and hope?

____

____

____

____

POINT 1

YOUR TESTIMONY SHOULD LEAD PEOPLE TO PRAISE GOD, NOT YOU

God is the star of a testimony. A person is the star of a biography.
—Tim Dilena

CONCEPT

A true testimony directs attention to God's mercy, not the storyteller's strength.

SCRIPTURE

+ Galatians 1:23–24: Paul's radical transformation led others to praise God.

ILLUSTRATION

+ The Rwandan man's worship and forgiveness pointed everyone to God's greatness.

DISCUSSION QUESTION

Do you tell your story in a way that highlights God as the main character?

____

____

POINT 2

YOUR TESTIMONY CRUSHES THE ENEMY'S LIES

CONCEPT

Speaking your story is spiritual warfare—it silences Satan's accusations.

SCRIPTURE

+ Revelation 12:11—Victory comes through the blood of Jesus and the word of testimony.

ILLUSTRATION

+ Travis and Radio's transformation in Detroit showed that no one is beyond redemption.

+ "Your testimony has Satan-defeating power. It crushes the enemy's number one weapon, his lies." —Tim Dilena

DISCUSSION QUESTION

What lies has the enemy used to silence you, and how can your testimony expose and defeat them?

____

____

POINT 3

YOUR TESTIMONY SILENCES CRITICS AND EMPOWERS BELIEVERS

CONCEPT

A changed life is undeniable—it shuts the mouths of skeptics and strengthens the Church.

SCRIPTURE

+ "We can't keep quiet about what we've seen and heard." (Acts 4:20)

ILLUSTRATION

+ Liam's miraculous healing in Amsterdam stirred faith and silenced doubt.

DISCUSSION QUESTION

What part of your story could silence doubt and give courage to others?

POINT 4

TESTIMONIES HAVE NO EXPIRATION DATE

> *You will be His witness to all people . . .* (Acts 22:15)

CONCEPT

God's work in your life never loses power—whether decades old or brand new, it's still relevant.

ILLUSTRATION

+ Nicky Cruz's decades-old testimony continues to change lives worldwide.

DISCUSSION QUESTION

Are there parts of your story you've stopped sharing because you thought they were too old or simple?

POINT 5

IT'S SIMPLE—DON'T COMPLICATE IT

CONCEPT

The power of your story is in its simplicity. "I was blind, but now I see."

SCRIPTURE

+ John 9:25—The blind man testified simply and powerfully.

ILLUSTRATION

+ The Olympic diver's salvation was sparked by a simple, remembered testimony.

DISCUSSION QUESTION

Do you ever feel pressure to make your story dramatic? How might God use its simplicity to reach someone?

____

____

____

CONCLUSION

Every believer's testimony is a weapon, a witness, and a gift. It points to God, defeats the enemy, silences critics, and never expires. Most of all, it's simple—just tell what Jesus has done for you.

CLOSING

Pray for boldness to tell your story with clarity and humility. Ask God to use your testimony to break lies, stir faith, and bring salvation.

Write out your testimony this week with Jesus at the center.

Pray for an opportunity to share it with someone who needs hope.

SPEAKING TO ETERNITY

Store up for yourselves treasures in heaven... For where your treasure is, there your heart will be also. (Matthew 6:19–21)

Every act of kindness, every gospel conversation, every moment of witness speaks to eternity—something God has already placed in the human heart (Ecclesiastes 3:11). We don't just speak to minds or opinions; we speak to the part of people that will live forever. That's why we fight "the good fight" (1 Timothy 6:12), not over trivialities, but to keep our joy, our anointing, and our freedom so that we can clearly declare eternal truths.

Tim Dilena challenged us to avoid shallow, trend-driven ministry and instead use eternal language, grounded in Scripture, to awaken the longing for God that already exists inside people. Eternity is too long to be wrong.

SCRIPTURES

+ "He has put eternity into man's heart." (Ecclesiastes 3:11)
+ "Fight the good fight for the true faith. Hold tightly to the eternal life . . ." (1 Timothy 6:12)

+ "The entirety of Your word is truth, and every one of Your righteous judgments endures forever." (Psalm 119:160)

+ "'One thing you lack . . . come, follow Me.'" (Mark 10:21)

QUOTES

+ "Only eternal language can be understood by the heart that has eternity set in it." —Tim Dilena

+ "Eternity is too long to be wrong." —Tim Dilena

+ "There are no ordinary people. It is immortals whom we joke with, work with, marry, snub, and exploit."[26] —C.S. Lewis

ILLUSTRATIONS

+ Helen Keller: Though blind and deaf, she said, "Thank you for telling me God's name, for He has touched me many times before."[27]

+ Ellie and the Nazi Guard: A Jewish woman's life was spared when a guard pointed her toward Jesus.

+ Pro Athlete in Church: Confronted with a sermon on hell, the eternal truth struck deeper than comfort.

If I find in myself a desire which no experience in this world can satisfy, the most probable explanation is that I was made for another world.[28] —C.S. Lewis

REFLECTION QUESTION

If eternity is already in people's hearts, what eternal words are you speaking into them?

POINT 1

ETERNITY IS ALREADY IN EVERY HEART

CONCEPT

Eternity isn't something we introduce; it's something God has already placed in every soul. Our role is to awaken it by speaking eternal truth, not just cultural commentary.

SCRIPTURE

+ He has put eternity into man's heart. (Ecclesiastes 3:11)

QUOTE

+ "There are no ordinary people. It is immortals whom we joke with, work with, marry, snub, and exploit."[29] —C.S. Lewis

ILLUSTRATION

+ Helen Keller's awareness of God before she even knew His name.

DISCUSSION QUESTIONS

How does knowing eternity is already in a person's heart change your approach to sharing Christ?

____

____

Can you recall a moment when God awakened something eternal in you before you even recognized it?

____

____

POINT 2

TRUTH IS THE LANGUAGE OF ETERNITY

> *The entirety of Your word is truth, and every one of Your righteous judgments endures forever.* (Psalm 119:160)

CONCEPT

The eternal heart understands one language—truth. God's Word transcends culture, politics, and time. Preaching trends may stir emotion, but only truth transforms.

QUOTE

+ "Always bring the Bible to bear on every heart. That is the sure way you can speak to eternity with an eternal language."
  —Tim Dilena

ILLUSTRATION

+ Tim Dilena's sermon on hell to a visiting pro athlete revealed how eternal truth resonates deeply.

DISCUSSION QUESTIONS

How does the eternal nature of Scripture give you confidence in difficult conversations?

____

____

____

When have you sensed the Spirit urging you to speak truth even when it was uncomfortable?

____

____

POINT 3

THE ETERNAL CONFRONTATION (WHEN THE GOOD TEACHER BECOMES GOD)

CONCEPT

Speaking to eternity often requires confrontation. Jesus' encounter with the rich young ruler showed that eternal truth forces people to choose: surrender or walk away.

> *One thing you lack: go and sell all you possess . . . and come, follow Me.* (Mark 10:21)

QUOTE

+ "It was all going great until the Good Teacher became God." —Tim Dilena

ILLUSTRATION

+ Jesus didn't lower the bar for the rich young ruler; He revealed the eternal cost of following Him.

DISCUSSION QUESTIONS

How can we speak truth in love when we know it might confront or offend?

___

___

___

What "one thing" might God be calling you to surrender to deepen your eternal witness?

___

CONCLUSION

Eternity is already inside every human heart. When we speak God's Word, we are awakening something planted by Him. Truth is the language eternity understands, and it often brings confrontation that leads to surrender. Eternity is too long to be wrong—so speak eternal words, live for eternal purposes, and fight for eternal impact.

CLOSING

Pray for a deeper awareness of eternity in every person you meet. Ask God to give you courage to speak truth with love, boldness, and clarity. Surrender your own "one thing" that may hinder eternal obedience.

Initiate One Eternity Conversation: Intentionally share an eternal truth with someone this week.

LIGHT VERSUS LIGHTNING

You are the light of the world. A city set on a hill cannot be hidden. (Matthew 5:14, ESV)

Most people will never read the Gospel of Matthew, Mark, Luke, or John—but they will read you. Gypsy Smith called Christians the "fifth Gospel," and the world forms its opinion of Jesus by watching His followers.[30] We often want lightning—moments of excitement, emotion, and impact—but God calls us to be steady light. Lightning is impressive; light is transformative. Evangelism isn't primarily what we say—it's who we are.

> *Lamps do not talk, but they do shine.*[31] —Charles Spurgeon

ILLUSTRATIONS

+ A college poll once asked, "What comes to mind when you hear the word Christianity?" The top answer: Christians don't practice what they preach. Light is not talk—it is consistency.

REFLECTION QUESTION

When people "read" your life, what do they see—lightning moments or steady light?

> *Let your light shine before others, that they may see your good deeds and glorify your Father in heaven.* (Matthew 5:16, NIV)

POINT 1

LIGHT, NOT LIGHTNING

CONCEPT

Lightning gets attention. It creates "oohs" and "ahhs." But it disappears in a moment. Light is steady, ordinary, and often unnoticed—but without it, nothing grows. God calls us not to be spiritual fireworks but daily lamps that stay on.

> *Lightning is impressive, but light is essential.* —Tim Dilena

SCRIPTURE

+ "For at one time you were darkness, but now you are light in the Lord. Walk as children of light." (Ephesians 5:8)

ILLUSTRATION

+ A room full of people do not cheer when the lights turn on—but they panic when the lights go out. Your faithfulness matters far more than your flare.

DISCUSSION QUESTIONS

Why is consistent light more powerful than occasional spiritual lightning?

What daily habits help keep your "light" on?

Where do you feel tempted to depend on lightning instead of steady obedience?

POINT 2

YOUR LIFE IS A SERMON

CONCEPT

Evangelism is not only conversation—it's demonstration. People watch how you respond to anger, pressure, interruptions, and injustice. Before they listen to our message, they examine our life.

> *There are five Gospels: Matthew, Mark, Luke, John, and the Christian, but most people never read the first four.*
> —Gypsy Smith[32]

SCRIPTURE

+ "Among whom you shine as lights in the world." (Philippians 2:15)

ILLUSTRATION

+ In a Middle Eastern restaurant, Tim Dilena simply showed kindness to the Yemeni servers. The unbelieving man with him said, "I've never seen anything like this." Light, not words, opened his heart.

DISCUSSION QUESTIONS

What part of your lifestyle speaks the loudest to unbelievers?

When has someone's example impacted you more than their words?

What simple act of light can you practice this week—kindness, patience, honesty, or gentleness?

POINT 3

THE CROSS SHOWS US HOW TO SHINE

CONCEPT

Peter points directly to Jesus on the cross as our model:

No retaliation.

No threats.

Entrusting Himself to the Father.

Our brightest moments often come through suffering, humility, and quiet obedience. Many are won to Christ "without a word."

SCRIPTURE

+ "While being reviled, He did not revile in return . . .He kept entrusting Himself to Him who judges righteously." (1 Peter 2:23)

ILLUSTRATION

+ The Roman centurion wasn't moved by Jesus' sermons—but by the way He died. His light under pressure opened the centurion's eyes: "Surely this man was the Son of God!" (Mark 15:39)

DISCUSSION QUESTION

Which of Jesus's responses on the cross challenges you most—no retaliation, no threats, or trusting the Father?

How can suffering or pressure actually make your light shine brighter?

Who in your life needs to "see" Jesus through your example rather than your words?

CONCLUSION

CONCEPT

Expose yourself to the Light—through Scripture, prayer, and obedience—and you will shine in darkness. You don't need to be exciting. You need to be consistent. *Lightning is impressive, but light transforms.*

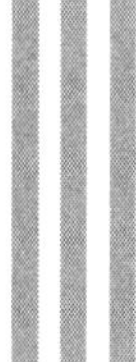

CLOSING

Pray that you shine where God is calling you—not with lightning, but with steady, faithful light.

16

REDEFINING VERY GOOD (GENESIS 2 MEANS ROUND 2 OF THE BIG FIGHT)

God created man in His own image . . . God saw all that He had made, and behold, it was very good. (Genesis 1:27–31, NASB)

There is a battle raging over what God declared "very good." Genesis 1 established God's authority as Creator, but the Genesis 2 battle strikes at gender, identity, and marriage. What began as a cultural skirmish is now a full-on spiritual war against the image of God imprinted on humanity.

Genesis 1 removed God; Genesis 2 replaces Him with man's opinions. What society calls progress, heaven calls rebellion. Yet God still speaks clearly and compassionately, calling His people to stand firm in truth and love. This is not just a cultural conversation, it's a spiritual confrontation. The Church must rise, not retreat.

> *If you are on the wrong road, progress means doing an about-turn . . .*[33] —C.S. Lewis

SCRIPTURES

+ Genesis 2:18–24: God institutes marriage between male and female.

+ "He who made them at the beginning made them male and female . . . No one should desecrate His art by cutting them apart." (Matthew 19:4–6, MSG/NKJV)

QUOTES

+ "When the Genesis 1 fight removed God, the Genesis 2 fight redefines man." —Tim Dilena

+ "Taking a stand draws attacks, but standing on truth draws Heaven." —Tim Dilena

+ "It's not about legal vs. illegal. It's about truth vs. deception." —Tim Dilena

+ "You don't have to compromise convictions to be compassionate."[34] —Rick Warren

+ "Once you abolish God, the government becomes God."[35] —G.K. Chesterton

ILLUSTRATION

+ The Scopes "Monkey Trial" (1925) symbolized the beginning of the Genesis 1 fight—removing the Creator from classrooms.[36] That battle paved the way for today's Genesis 2 fight—redefining humanity itself. When the Creator is dismissed, confusion follows.

POINT 1

WHY HAS THIS PEOPLE BACKSLIDDEN?

CONCEPT

The first sign of spiritual collapse is a refusal to repent. When God's Word is rejected, morality is rewritten, and deception is legislated as truth. Rebellion deepens when people say, "What have I done?" instead of confessing sin.

SCRIPTURES

+ "No man repented of his wickedness, saying, 'What have I done?' Everyone turned to his own course . . ." (Jeremiah 8:5–6, NKJV)

+ "Since they have rejected the word of the Lord, what kind of wisdom do they have?" (Jeremiah 8:8–9, NIV)

ILLUSTRATION

+ A Catholic priest once told Tim Dilena's children that Genesis 1–3 was allegory. But if Genesis is a myth, then so is sin, and so is the Savior. Spiritual deception often hides in religious garb.

People assume that just because it's a law, God accepts it. But truth has no expiration date. —Tim Dilena

DISCUSSION QUESTIONS

Have you ever been deceived by something that sounded "right" but wasn't biblical? How did God break through that deception?

____

____

When God convicts you of sin, do you respond with defensiveness, indifference, or surrender? What does that reveal about who has authority in your life?

____

____

POINT 2

WHY ARE WE SITTING HERE?

> *Taking a stand draws attacks, but standing on truth draws Heaven.* —Tim Dilena

CONCEPT

Jeremiah challenged a passive people who sat still in crisis. Likewise, the Church cannot stay silent while culture redefines truth. Silence isn't neutrality—it's surrender. Taking a stand may invite fire, but it also invites Christ's presence.

SCRIPTURES

+ "Why do we sit still? Assemble yourselves . . ." (Jeremiah 8:14, KJV)

+ "You are to influence them, not let them influence you!" (Jeremiah 15:19, TLB)

ILLUSTRATION

+ The Hebrew boys in Daniel 3 met Jesus not when they refused to bow, but when they were thrown into the furnace. Standing invites attacks, but it guarantees God's presence.

DISCUSSION QUESTIONS

What has fear of rejection or cancellation kept you from saying or doing in faith?

When obedience to God has cost you something, how did He meet you in the fire?

____

____

____

POINT 3

WHY HAS THEIR HEALTH NOT BEEN RESTORED?

CONCEPT

Healing fails when leaders and people compromise truth. God's Word cannot bring restoration where it is softened, silenced, or replaced with comfort. We cannot heal what we refuse to confront.

SCRIPTURES

+ "Is there no balm in Gilead . . . Why then is there no recovery for the health of the daughter of my people?" (Jeremiah 8:22, NKJV)

+ "Only if you return to trusting Me will I let you continue as My spokesman . . ." (Jeremiah 15:19–21, TLB)

ILLUSTRATION

+ Sermons were removed from social media platforms for "violating norms," though no rules were broken. The battle over truth isn't just theological—it's digital. Even algorithms oppose righteousness, but God's Word still stands.

We cannot let the world influence the pulpit. We are called to influence them. —Tim Dilena

DISCUSSION QUESTIONS

What spiritual conditions in your community burden you most? How might God be calling you to step into the gap?

How has God's truth brought real healing in your life? How can your story bring hope to others?

CLOSING

Spend time praying over identity, yours and others. Ask the Holy Spirit to expose every lie that culture, fear, or past pain has whispered. Intercede for the Church to rise with compassion and courage in the Genesis 2 battle. Ask for boldness to speak truth without compromise and for a supernatural love that restores the broken. Invite Jesus to restore what's been stolen through deception and to affirm who He says we are.

NOTES

CHAPTER 1

1 Brennan Manning, *The Ragamuffin Gospel: Good News for the Bedraggled, Beat-Up, and Burnt Out* (Colorado Springs, CO: Multnomah Books, 1990), 102.

2 Brian L. Powell, "Duck Church," *Brian L Powell* (blog), October 30, 2015, https://brianlpowell.com/2015/10/30/duck-church/.

CHAPTER 2

3 Charles H. Spurgeon, "The Lover of God's Law Filled with Peace" (sermon, New Park Street Pulpit, London, January 1888), in *The Metropolitan Tabernacle Pulpit: Sermons Preached by C. H. Spurgeon, vol. 34* (London: Passmore & Alabaster, 1888), 65–72.

4 David W. Music, "History of Hymns: 'I Have Decided to Follow Jesus'," Discipleship Ministries, June 10, 2020, https://www.umcdiscipleship.org/articles/history of hymns i-have-decided-to-follow-jesus.

CHAPTER 3

5 John Wesley, "Twelve Rules of a Helper," in *The Works of John Wesley, vol. 14, Journals and Diaries V* (1765–1775), ed. W. Reginald Ward and Richard P. Heitzenrater (Nashville: Abingdon Press, 1993), 281.

CHAPTER 4

6 "Lincoln Frees a Slave," *Preaching Today,* accessed November 18, 2025, https://www.preachingtoday.com/illustrations/2001/july/13140.html.

7 As cited in Tony Cooke, "Acts 3: The Validating Chapter," *Tony Cooke Ministries*, accessed October 7, 2025, https://tonycooke.org/articles-by-tony-cooke/acts-3-the-validating-chapter/. The maxim holds that the miraculous power in Acts 3 validates the spiritual experience in Acts 2.

8 D.L. Moody, "I like my way of doing it better than your way of not doing it," quoted in Tony Cooke, "D. L. Moody's Conversion and Rough Start," Tony Cooke Ministries, October 13, 2023, https://tonycooke.org/articles-by-tony-cooke/d-l-moodys-conversion-and-rough-start/.

9 William Revell Moody, *The Life of D.L. Moody* (New York: Fleming H. Revell, 1900), 146.

10 David Wilkerson, with John and Elizabeth Sherrill, *The Cross and the Switchblade* (New York: Random House, 1963), 8-9.

NOTES

CHAPTER 5

11 See Sonny Arguinzoni Sr., *Treasures Out of Darkness.* (La Puente, CA: Victory Outreach Pub., 1996).

12 *We Bought a Zoo*, directed by Cameron Crowe (Beverly Hills, CA: 20th Century Fox, 2011), Film.

13 Steve Jobs, quoted in John Sculley and John A. Byrne, *Odyssey: Pepsi to Apple: A Journey of Adventure, Ideas, and the Future* (New York: Harper & Row, 1987), 170.

CHAPTER 6

14 Francis S. Collins, *The Language of God: A Scientist Presents Evidence for Belief* (New York: Free Press, 2006), 17.

15 See Erwin W. Lutzer, "John Harper's Last Convert," Moody Church Media (Moody Church, n.d.), accessed November 23, 2025, https://www.moodymedia.org/articles/sharing-gift-christmas-one-minute-you-die/.

CHAPTER 7

16 "The Hebrides Revival," *Christians Together*, accessed November 18, 2025, https://www.christianstogether.net/Articles/94936/Revival_in_the.aspx.

CHAPTER 8

17 "Garbage Barge Mobro Cruises U.S. Atlantic and Gulf Coasts," *EBSCO Information Services, Inc.*, accessed September 30, 2025, https://www.ebsco.com/research-starters/history/garbage-barge-mobro-cruises-usatlantic-and-gulf-coasts.

CHAPTER 9

18 Lee Strobel, *The Case for Faith: A Journalist Investigates the Toughest Objections to Christianity* (Grand Rapids, MI: Zondervan Publishing, 2000), 71.

19 Strobel, *Case for Faith*, 71.

CHAPTER 10

20 Moody Bible Institute, "D. L. Moody's Story," accessed November 21, 2025, https://www.moodybible.org/about/d-l-moody/.

21 O.S. Hawkins and Matt Queen, *The Gospel Invitation: Why Publicly Inviting People to Receive Christ Still Matters* (Nashville, TN: Thomas Nelson, (2023), Kindle.

22 Gordon-Conwell Theological Seminary, "Status of Global Christianity, 2025, in the Context of 1900 –2050," Center for the Study of Global Christianity, January 2025, accessed October 10, 2025, https://www.gordonconwell.edu/wp-content/uploads/sites/13/2025/01/Status-of-Global-Christianity-2025.pdf.

CHAPTER 11

23 William Booth, quoted in Harold Begbie, *The Life of General William Booth: The Founder of the Salvation Army, vol. 1* (New York: The Macmillan Company, 1920), discusses this theme at length.

24 John Wesley, *The Journal of the Rev. John Wesley, A.M.*, ed. Nehemiah Curnock, 8 vols. (London: Charles H. Kelly, 1909–1916), 4:87.

CHAPTER 12

25 Victor Hugo, *Things Seen*, trans. Stephen Grant (New York: Henry Holt, 2012), 175.

CHAPTER 14

26 C.S. Lewis, "The Weight of Glory," in *The Weight of Glory and Other Addresses*, rev. and exp. ed. (New York: HarperCollins, 2001), 46.

27 Ferdinand Funk, "The Story Is Told That After Helen Kellers," SermonCentral, September 26, 2008, https://www.sermoncentral.com/sermon-illustrations/69045/the-story-is-told-that-after-helen-keller-s-by-ferdinand-funk.

28 C.S. Lewis, *Mere Christianity* (New York: HarperCollins, 2001), 136–37.

29 C.S. Lewis, *Weight of Glory*, 46.

CHAPTER 15

30 Bobby Conway, "The Fifth Gospel: The Ultimate Apologetic," *Christian Research Institute*, updated April 12, 2023, https://www.equip.org/ articles/fifth-gospel-ultimate-apologetic/.

31 Charles Haddon Spurgeon, *"The Clean and the Unclean"* 1863, The Spurgeon Center, accessed August 26, 2025. https://www.spurgeon.org/ resource-library/sermons/the-clean-and-the-unclean/#flipbook/.

32 Conway, "The Fifth Gospel," *Christian Research Institute.*

CHAPTER 16

33 C.S. Lewis, *Mere Christianity*, 38.

34 Rick Warren, quoted in Brandon A. Cox, "EXCLUSIVE Rick Warren: 'Flat Out Wrong' That Muslims, Christians View God the Same," *The Christian Post*, March 2, 2012, www.christianpost.com.

35 Gilbert K. Chesterton, *Christendom in Dublin* (London: Sheed & Ward, 1932), chapter 3.

36 Mindy Johnston, *"Scopes Trial,"* Encyclopaedia Britannica, last modified July 21, 2025, https://www.britannica.com/event/Scopes-Trial.

ALSO AVAILABLE

FROM TIM DILENA

GET INSIGHT

Discover life-changing lessons from each New Testament chapter, one day at a time.

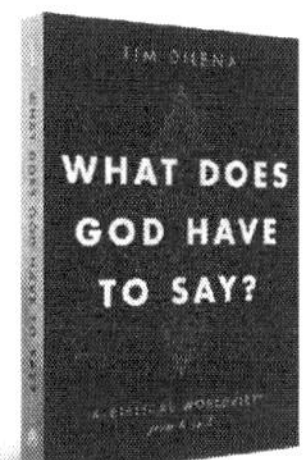

STAND FIRM

Learn God's principles to hold steady in an unstable world.

TRUST GOD

See how God can lead you through life's ups and downs.

LEARN TO PRAY

Discover 101 ways to talk to God about your struggles, like fear, forgiveness, anxiety and more.

DON'T GIVE UP

Nurture a daily mindset to keep you moving forward in life and in faith.

BREAK THROUGH

Experience how the power of prayer can change everything.

For more spiritual insight to help you thrive in everyday life:

Explore
messages and books at
tsc.nyc

Follow us

@TimesSquareChurch

@PastorTimDilena

TIMES SQUARE CHURCH

1657 Broadway NY, NY 10019
tsc.nyc